Let's Make Bracelets

Tips & Techniques for Fabulous Fun

By Joe Gannon

Projects by Raffaella Dowling

Mud Puddle inc.

NEW YORK

Let's Make Bracelets:
Tips & Techniques
for Fabulous Fun
by Joe Gannon
projects by Rafaella Dowling

Copyright © 2010 by
Mud Puddle Books, Inc.
54 W. 21st Street Suite 601
New York, NY 10010
info@mudpuddlebooks.com

ISBN: 978-1-60311-247-5

The friendship bracelets on pages 36-47 were originally published in
Beaded Friendship Bracelets by Kaylee Connor © 2008 by Mud Puddle Books.

Printed in China

Contents

Introduction

MAKING your own bracelets can be fun, easy, and inexpensive. You can make as many as you like! Fill your jewelry box with variations to suit your every mood. Make beautiful gifts for your friends. Produce interesting theme bracelets for parties, holidays, or any other occasion. Use hearts for Valentine's Day, shamrocks for St. Patrick's Day, stars and stripes for the Fourth of July, or candles for your birthday. Make them simple or ornate, casual or dressy. Use your creativity and ingenuity to design fabulous wrist wear.

The materials can be scraps from your sewing kit: thread, ribbons, buttons, safety pins, and strips of fabric—or from your desk: rubber bands, scrap paper, glue, and paste. Foam sheets and strips, precut foam shapes, embroidery floss, Velcro, and pony beads are all available at almost any craft store. Use the examples here to get you started, then let your imagination run wild designing and making fun bracelets for yourself and all your friends.

Supplies

foam straps or sheets

foam die cut shapes

thread or embroidery floss

buttons

lanyard

beads

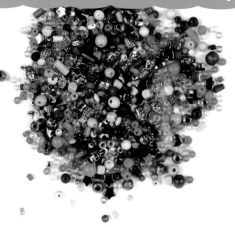

Fastener Tape
(such as Velcro®)

safety pins

glue

Snake Bracelet

1. Use a tape measure wrapped around your wrist to determine how long your snake bracelet needs to be. Don't make it too tight and be sure to allow an overlap for the bracelet's closure.

2. Draw the outline of the snake on a foam strap or sheet. Then, cut it out with scissors.

3. Draw the tongue, tail, and decorative stripes on contrasting colors of foam. Cut them out as well.

4. The snake's eyes can be round, square, oval or triangular and should be cut from a white or light-colored foam. Add pupils to the eyes using a permanent marker.

You'll Need:

- Foam sheets or strips
- Fastener tape
- Marker
- Scissors
- Glue

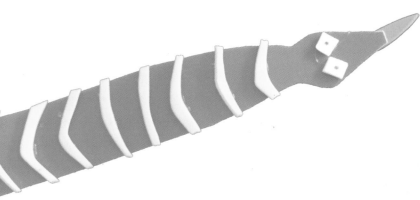

5. Glue the tongue, tail, decorative stripes, and eyes to the body of the snake.

6. Glue one small strip of fastener tape just in front of the snakes tail. Then, glue a small strip of fastener tape to the back of the snake's head, so that when the two strips of fastener tape are attached to each other the snake bracelet will be held closed.

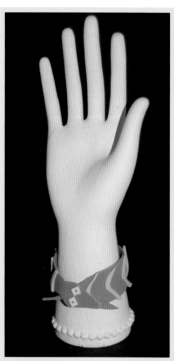

Flower Dot Bracelet

1. Use a tape measure wrapped around your wrist to determine how long your flower dot bracelet needs to be. Don't make it too tight and be sure to allow an overlap for the bracelet's closure.

2. Measure and draw a strap for your bracelet on a foam strip or sheet. Then, cut it out with scissors.

3. Draw a large flower shape, a smaller flower shape, and an even smaller flower shape on contrasting colors of foam. Cut them out as well. If you have appropriate precut foam shapes feel free to use them instead.

4. A dot for the center of the main flower should be cut from a contrasting color of foam. Several more dots should be cut

You'll Need:

- Foam sheets or strips
- Fastener tape
- Marker
- Scissors
- Glue

out to decorate the bracelet. Again, precut dots can be used if you have them.

5. Glue the three flower shapes together with the largest on the bottom, and then glue a dot in the center.

6. Glue the large flower assembly to the center of the band, then glue on the other dots as well to decorate the sides of the band.

7. Glue one small strip of fastener tape near one end of the front (outside) of the bracelet strap. Then, glue a small strip of fastener tape to the back of the other end so that when the two strips attach to each other the bracelet will be held closed.

11

Star Cuff

1. Use a tape measure wrapped around your wrist to determine how long your star cuff bracelet band needs to be. Don't make it too tight and be sure to allow an overlap for the bracelet's closure.

2. Measure and draw out a strap for your bracelet on a foam strip or sheet roughly following the strap shape shown. Then, cut it out with scissors.

3. Draw a large star shape and several smaller ones. Cut them out as well. If you have appropriate precut foam shapes feel free to use them instead.

4. Cut out several dots from a contrasting color of foam to decorate the

You'll Need:

- Foam sheets or strips
- Fastener tape
- Marker
- Scissors
- Glue

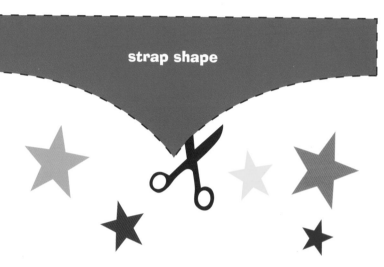

strap shape

bracelet. Again, precut dots can be used if you have them.

5. Glue a large central star in the middle of the band, then glue the smaller stars and dots decoratively around the sides of the bracelet.

6. Glue one small strip of fastener tape near one end of the front (outside) of the bracelet strap. Then, glue a small strip of fastener tape to the back of the other end so that when the two strips attach to each other the bracelet will be held closed.

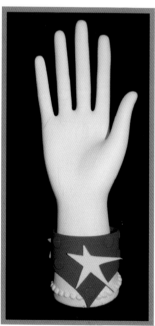

Flower Vine

1. Use a tape measure wrapped around your wrist to determine how long your bracelet needs to be. Don't make it too tight and be sure to allow an overlap for the bracelet's closure.

2. Measure and draw out a strap for your bracelet on a green foam strip or sheet. Then, cut it out with scissors.

3. Draw four or five flower shapes— enough to decorate all of the way around the strap— and cut them out as well. If you have appropriate precut foam shapes, feel free to use them instead.

4. A dot for the center of each flower should be cut from a contrasting color of foam. Again, precut dots can be used if you have them. Glue the dots in the center of each flower.

You'll Need:

- Foam sheets or strips
- Fastener tape
- Marker
- Scissors
- Glue

14

5. Draw some leaves on the same green color foam as the strap and cut them out.

6. Glue the flower shapes onto the strap staggering them up and down around the strap as if they were on a vine.

7. Glue the leaves onto the inside surface of the strap so they stick out from the edges like leaves on a vine.

8. Glue one small strip of fastener tape near one end of the front (outside) of the bracelet strap. Then, glue a small strip of fastener tape to the back of the other end so that when the two strips attach to each other the bracelet will be held closed.

Hearts on Your Sleeve

1. Use a tape measure wrapped around your wrist to determine how long your bracelet needs to be. Don't make it too tight and be sure to allow an overlap for the bracelet's closure.

2. Measure and draw out a strap for your bracelet on a foam strip or sheet. Then, cut out the bracelet strap with scissors.

3. Draw an assortment of large and small heart shapes— enough to decorate all of the way around the strap—and cut them out as well. If you have appropriate precut foam shapes feel free to use them instead.

4. For the larger heart shapes draw and cut out a smaller heart to decorate the center. Glue the smaller hearts in the center of each larger one.

You'll Need:

- Foam sheets or strips
- Fastener tape
- Marker
- Scissors
- Glue

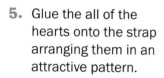

5. Glue the all of the hearts onto the strap arranging them in an attractive pattern.

6. Glue one small strip of fastener tape near one end of the front (outside) of the bracelet strap. Then, glue a small strip of fastener tape to the back of the other end so that when the two strips attach to each other the bracelet will be held closed.

Paper Roll Bead String

1. Use a tape measure wrapped around your wrist to determine how long your bracelet needs to be. Don't make it too tight and be sure to allow enough slack for a comfortable fit.

2. Select some decorative papers for making the beads. Leftover scraps of wrapping paper, comic strips from the Sunday paper, or glossy photo pages from magazines all make great sources of paper for your bracelet beads.

3. Cut the paper into strips about 2 inches (50 mm) wide by 2½ inches (64 mm) long and roll the strip around the pencil or dowel.

4. Glue the end of the strip down to the paper roll and slide it off of the pencil. Add some extra glue all around the edges of the paper at the ends of the bead.

You'll Need:

- Decorative paper
- Elastic string
- Scissors
- A pencil or dowel
- Glue or paste

thread the elastic
string through the
beads in opposite
directions

5. Arrange the beads in a row
and keep adding beads until
you have enough to fill the
length of bracelet that you
measured in step one.

6. Thread the elastic string up
through one bead and down
through the next until it is
extending from the last bead
in the row—leave enough at
both ends for tying a knot.
Repeat the procedure going
back through the beads in
the opposite direction.

7. Now, knot the ends of the
string together to finish your
bracelet. It will help to have a
friend hold the bracelet while
you tie. For a cleaner look you
can slide the thread through
the beads so that the knots
disappear inside them.

Small Roll Bead String

1. Use a tape measure wrapped around your wrist to determine how long your bracelet needs to be. Don't make it too tight and be sure to allow enough slack for a comfortable fit.

2. Select some decorative papers for making the beads. Leftover scraps of wrapping paper, comic strips from the Sunday paper, or glossy photo pages from magazines all make great sources of paper for your bracelet beads.

3. Cut the paper into strips about 1 inch (25 mm) wide by 2½ inches (64 mm) long and roll the strip around the pencil or dowel.

4. Glue the end of the strip down to the paper roll and slide it off of the pencil. Add some extra glue all around the edges of the paper at the ends of the bead.

You'll Need:

- Decorative paper
- Elastic string
- Scissors
- A pencil or dowel
- Glue or paste

5. Arrange the beads in a row and keep adding beads until you have enough to fill the length of bracelet that you measured in step one.

6. Thread the elastic string up through one bead and down through the next until it is extending from the last bead in the row—leave enough at both ends for tying a knot. Repeat the procedure going back through the beads in the opposite direction.

7. Now, knot the ends of the string together to finish your bracelet. It will help to have a friend hold the bracelet while you tie. For a cleaner look you can slide the thread through the beads so that the knots disappear inside them.

Safety Pin Beaded Bracelet

1. Use a tape measure wrapped around your wrist to determine how long your bracelet needs to be. Don't make it too tight and be sure to allow enough slack for a comfortable fit.

2. Decide which colors and patterns you will use in placing the beads on the safety pins.

3. Unclasp a safety pin and place enough beads on the open prong to fill the its length once it is closed.

4. Reclasp the safety pin and repeat the process on enough safety pins to make up the full length of your bracelet.

5. Cut two lengths of elastic string to the measurement determined in step one plus enough extra to easily tie the ends together—about three extra inches (76 mm) should be plenty.

You'll Need:

- Safety Pins
- Beads
- Elastic string
- Scissors

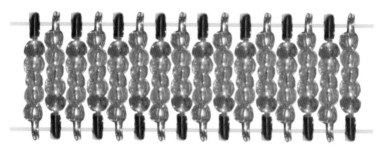

alternate the safety pins head-up then head-down
as you string them on the elastic cord

6. Temporarily tie an extra
bead to the end of each
string to keep the safety
pins from falling off while
you string them. Then,
thread the strings through
the ends of the safety
pins to form your bracelet.
Alternate the pins head-up
then head-down so that
they will line up evenly.

7. Now remove the temporary
bead and knot the ends of
the elastic string together
to finish your bracelet. It
will help to have a friend
hold the bracelet while you
tie the strings.

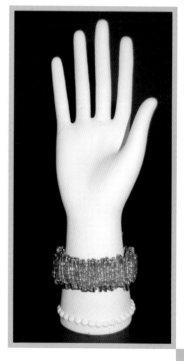

Button Jewel Bracelet

1. Use a tape measure wrapped around your wrist to determine how long your bracelet needs to be. Don't make it too tight and be sure to allow enough slack for a comfortable fit.

2. Decide which colors and patterns you will use in arranging the buttons in your bracelet.

3. Stack up the large, medium, and small buttons you will be using for your central jewel.

4. Lay out the buttons for your band to make sure you have enough to fill the length of your bracelet.

You'll Need:

- A large button
- A medium button
- Several smaller buttons
- Elastic string
- Scissors

5. Cut a length of elastic string to about twice the measurement determined in step one. This should allow for stitching and tying off.

thread through all three buttons to make the jewel

overlap the buttons to make the band

6. Thread the elastic string through the holes in the three buttons of your jewel. Pull the string through until the jewel is in the center of the string.

7. Now thread on the buttons that make up the band layering them in overlapping an fashion.

8. When you have enough buttons in the band to match the measurement from step one, tie off the elastic to complete your bracelet. It will help to have a friend hold the bracelet while you tie the string. Make the knot on the back of the band so that it is hidden when the bracelet is being worn.

Layered Button Bangle

1. Use a tape measure wrapped around your wrist to determine how long your bracelet needs to be. Don't make it too tight and be sure to allow enough slack for a comfortable fit.

2. Decide which colors and patterns you will use in arranging the buttons in your bracelet.

3. Lay out the buttons for your band to make sure you have enough to fill the length of your bracelet.

4. Cut a length of elastic string to about twice the measurement determined in step one. This should allow enough for stitching and tying off.

You'll Need:

- Several large buttons
- Several smaller buttons
- Elastic string
- Scissors

5. Thread the elastic string through the holes in one of the large buttons and pull the

**insert regularly spaced large buttons between
sequences of smaller ones**

string through until the
button is in the center of
the string.

6. Now thread the smaller
buttons that separate
the larger ones in the
bracelet. These smaller
button sequences should
all be of matching lengths.
Make the full length of the
bracelet by layering them
in an overlapping fashion.

7. When you have enough
buttons in the band to
match the measurement
from step one, tie off the
elastic to complete your
bracelet. It will help to have
a friend hold the bracelet
while you tie the string.
Make the knot on the back
of the band so that it is
hidden when the bracelet
is being worn.

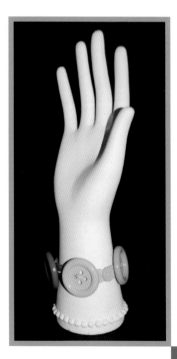

Rubber Band Chain

1. Use a tape measure wrapped around your wrist to determine how long your bracelet needs to be. Don't make it too tight and be sure to allow enough slack for a comfortable fit.

2. Decide which colors and patterns you will use in arranging the rubber bands in your bracelet.

3. Lay out the rubber bands for your bracelet to make sure you have enough to fill the length that you measured in step one, plus a couple of inches.

4. To start your chain, place the end of one rubber band through loop of another and fold it back on itself. Pull the remaining end of the rubber band back through the loop created by folding its end back

You'll Need:

• Several rubber bands in assorted colors.

to make a rubber band chain insert one of the rubber bands through the other and then loop it back through itself and pull it tight, repeat with the next rubber band, and so on . . .

on itself. It should look like the picture at the top of this page. Then pull it tight to form the first pair of *links* in your chain.

5. Repeat this process with another rubber band to form a chain of three. Keep on repeating until your chain reaches the length measured in step one, plus about two inches (50 mm) to give you some slack for tying the ends together.

6. Tie off the ends using a nice snug square knot to finish your bracelet.

Rubber Band Braid

1. Use a tape measure wrapped around your wrist to determine how long your bracelet needs to be. Don't make it too tight and be sure to allow enough slack for a comfortable fit.

2. Lay out some rubber bands end to end in three rows. Make sure you have enough to fill the length that you measured in step one, plus plenty of extra to allow for the length lost in braiding.

3. Loop your rubber bands together to form three rubber band chains as described on pages 28–29.

4. Pass a pencil (or similar stick) through one end of each of the chains to anchor them while you braid. Lay the chains down on a flat surface. Each chain will be a strand in your braid.

You'll Need:

- Several rubber bands in assorted colors.

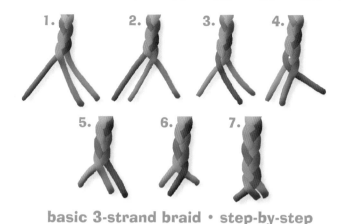

basic 3-strand braid • step-by-step

5. Take the strand on the right and pass it over the center strand. It now becomes the center strand. Then, take the strand on the left and pass it over the center strand. Keep alternating the right strand over the center, then the left strand over the new center, and so on, to form your braid. Snug up the braid as you go to keep it neat.

6. When you have reached the desired length, tie off the ends using a nice snug square knot to finish your bracelet.

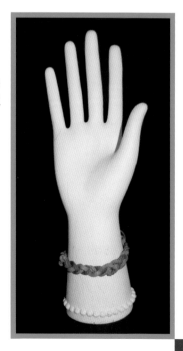

Pony Bead Strand

1. Use a tape measure wrapped around your wrist to determine how long your bracelet needs to be. Don't make it too tight and be sure to allow enough slack for a comfortable fit.

2. Decide which colors and patterns you will use in arranging the pony beads in your bracelet.

3. Lay out the beads for your bracelet on a flat surface to make sure you like the pattern and have enough to fill the length that you measured in step one.

4. To start your bracelet, thread the elastic string up through one row of beads and down through the next until it is extending from the last

You'll Need:

- An assortment of pony beads in various colors
- Elastic string
- Scissors

thread the elastic string through the rows of beads in opposite directions

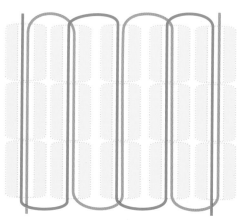

bead in the final row—leave enough at both ends for tying a knot.

5. Repeat the procedure going back through the beads in the opposite direction.

6. Now, knot the ends of the string together to finish your bracelet. It will help to have a friend hold the bracelet while you tie. For a cleaner look you can slide the threads through the beads so that the knots disappear inside them.

Pony Bead Diamond

1. Use a tape measure wrapped around your wrist to determine how long your bracelet needs to be. Don't make it too tight and be sure to allow enough slack for a comfortable fit.

2. Decide which colors and patterns you would like to use in arranging the pony beads in your bracelet.

3. Lay out the beads for your bracelet on a flat surface to make sure you like the colors and pattern and have enough to fill the length that you measured in step one. There should be seven beads in the center row, then six in each of the rows neighboring it, then five in the next, and finally four in each of the rows for the rest of the bracelet.

You'll Need:

- An assortment of pony beads in various colors
- Elastic string
- Scissors

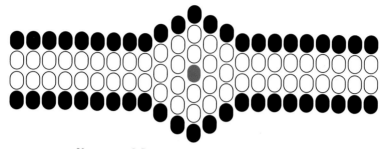

**diamond bracelet bead pattern,
vary the colors to suit your taste**

4. To start, thread the elastic string up through one row of beads and down through the next until it is extending from the last bead in the final row—leave enough at both ends for tying a knot.

5. Repeat the procedure going back through the beads in the opposite direction.

6. Now, knot the ends of the strings together to finish your bracelet. It will help to have a friend hold the bracelet while you tie. For a cleaner look you can slide the threads through the beads so that the knots disappear inside them.

Friendship Bracelet Knots

There are 3 basic knots used to make friendship bracelets in this book. They are easy to master and easy to remember, but you may want to practice a little before beginning to make your first friendship bracelet. A little practice now will save a considerable amount of frustration, time, and materials.

Overhand Knots

This knot can be created with as few as 2 threads, but you can use as many threads as you like.

Right Overhand Knot
Step 1

Measure at least 2 threads to be 4 times the length of the finished bracelet. (Double the length if you will be folding the threads in half before you start knotting.)

Tightly hold the left-hand thread and knot the remaining thread around it.

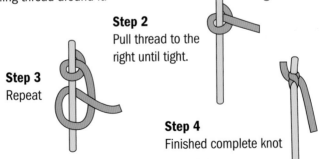

Step 2
Pull thread to the right until tight.

Step 3
Repeat

Step 4
Finished complete knot

Reminder: *A complete overhand knot is always tied twice.*

Left Overhand Knot
Step 1
Measure at least 2 threads to be 4 times the length of the finished bracelet. (Double the length if you will be folding the threads in half before you start knotting.)

Tightly hold the right-hand thread and knot the remaining thread around it.

Step 3
Repeat

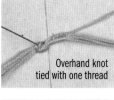

Step 2
Pull thread to the left until tight.

Step 4
Finished complete knot

Notes:

1. In this book the overhand knot is sometimes completed as a right overhand knot and sometimes as a left overhand knot, but either way it is the same knot.

2. The overhand knot can be made with as many threads as you want.

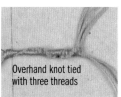

Overhand knot tied with one thread

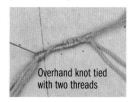

Overhand knot tied with two threads

Overhand knot tied with three threads

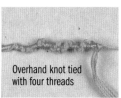

Overhand knot tied with four threads

Square Knot

Step 1

Measure each of 4 strands to be 4 times the desired length of the finished bracelet. Knot the strands together at one end, and pin the knot to a knotting board. Separate the strands.

Step 2

Move thread #4 from the far right and cross it over the center threads (#2 and #3) and under thread #1.

Step 3

Move thread #1 over thread #4 and under threads #2 and #3.

Step 4

Bring thread #1 from behind through the loop in thread #4 (far right).

Step 5
Pull on threads #1 and #4 to create the first half of the square knot.

Step 6
Move thread #4 from the left and cross it over the center strands (#2 and #3) and under thread #1.

Step 7
Bring thread #1 under threads #2 and #3 and through the loop on the far left.

Step 8
Pull on threads #1 and #4 to finish the square knot.

Ending Your Bracelet

Each of the projects in this book tells how to end the bracelet as it is pictured in the example. However, the following endings can be used with any of the bracelets you learn to make, so feel free to make any substitutions.

Possibility 1: Looped-End Bracelet

Folding the threads in half when starting the bracelet will create a loop at one end that can be used for tying bracelet ends together.

To Wear:
Wrap the finished bracelet around your wrist. Divide the threads at the loose end, and slip one half the threads through the loop. Tie to the other half of the threads, securing in a double knot so that the bracelet does not come untied.

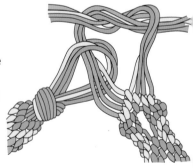

Possibility 2: Loose-Ends Bracelet

This bracelet is made by using single strands of thread that are not folded in half and looped.

To Wear:
Wrap the finished bracelet around your wrist. Tie ends together in a double knot, cutting longer ends to desired length.

Possibility 3: Jewelry Closure Bracelet

These bracelets have jewelry closures at both ends just like traditional jewelry, making it possible to remove the bracelet as often as desired.

The closures are easiest to attach when the bracelet is made from 3 or 4 strands of embroidery floss. After tying the closures to the bracelet ends, you may need to place a small amount of fabric glue over the knots to keep them secure.

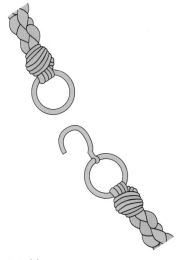

To Wear:
Attach this bracelet to your wrist just as you would attach any piece of traditional jewelry.

Basic Wrapped Bracelet

This easy bracelet requires a flexible core thread to wrap the threads of the bracelet around. Mix up the size of your bracelets by using a thin or thick core—and wear them singly or all together.

You'll Need:

- Core thread, thin
- Embroidery floss, 1 color
- Scissors

1. Cut core thread to desired length of finished bracelet plus a little for finishing. Cut 2 strands of embroidery floss to 4 times the length of the core thread, tie both strands of floss to the core. Be sure to leave a long enough tail to tie your bracelet onto your wrist.

2. Pin the core thread to the knotting board. Tightly wrap both strands of floss around the core thread to the end and tie in a knot.

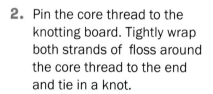

3. Wrap finished bracelet around wrist and tie floss ends together in a double knot. If ends are too long, trim to desired length.

Wrapped Bracelet with Alternating Colors

Want to add a little variety to your wrapped bracelets? This simple bracelet alternates colors to let you and your friends show off your school colors, your club colors, or just your favorite colors.

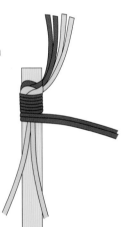

1. Cut core thread to desired length of finished bracelet plus a little for finishing. Cut 2 strands of each color embroidery floss to 4 times the length of the core thread, tie all strands of floss to the core. Be sure to leave a long enough tail to tie your bracelet onto your wrist.

2. Pin the core thread to the knotting board. Tightly wrap the 2 strands of the first color of floss around the core and the second color of floss until you have the desired amount of color.

You'll Need:

- Core thread, thin
- Embroidery floss, 2 colors
- Scissors

3. Pick up the strands of the second color floss and tightly wrap around both the core thread and the first color of floss until you have the desired amount of color.

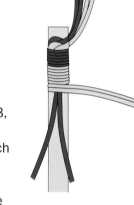

4. Repeat Steps 2 and 3, alternating colors as desired until you reach the end of the core thread. Knot tightly at the end of the core thread.

5. Wrap finished bracelet around wrist and tie floss ends together in a double knot. If ends are too long, trim to desired length.

Wrapped Bracelet with Twisted Thread

1. Cut core thread to desired length of finished bracelet plus a little for finishing. Cut 2 strands of embroidery floss and 2 strands of thin cord to 4 times the length of the core thread, tie both strands of floss to the core. Be sure to leave a long enough tail to tie your bracelet onto your wrist.

2. Tie thin cord to the core thread directly beneath the floss.

3. Pin the core thread to the Knotting Board. Wrap the 2 embroidery floss strands around the core thread and thin cords for about ½" (1.3 cm).

You'll Need:

- Core thread, thick
- Thin cord, 1 color
- Embroidery floss, 1 color
- Scissors